Original title:
Living with Leaves

Copyright © 2025 Creative Arts Management OÜ
All rights reserved.

Author: Isabella Rosemont
ISBN HARDBACK: 978-1-80581-803-8
ISBN PAPERBACK: 978-1-80581-330-9
ISBN EBOOK: 978-1-80581-803-8

Beneath the Branches

Beneath the branches, I find my shoes,
All mismatched and covered in blues.
The squirrels have taken my lunch away,
Laughing and chattering, they join the play.

Leaves rain down like confetti bright,
I dodge and I weave, it's quite the sight.
One smacks my head, oh what a tease,
The trees just chuckle, swaying with ease.

Autumn's Embrace

Autumn's hug is a little too tight,
I'm stuck in a jacket, it doesn't feel right.
I trip on a leaf, that sneaky old thing,
It giggles in whispers, does a little fling.

Pumpkin spice lattes, they call my name,
But I roast my tongue, oh what a shame.
Neighbors all shout for their rakes and their brooms,
While I dance in the wind, avoiding the gloom.

The Language of Foliage

The trees have secrets, they gossip away,
About all the critters that come out to play.
A whisper of rustle, a rustle of cheer,
They share all their stories for all who can hear.

Maples are sassy, oaks hold their ground,
Pines stand tall, never make a sound.
I eavesdrop here with an ear to the bark,
But the birch just giggles, it's always a lark!

Shadows of the Arboreal

In shadows of trees, I find my lost key,
The owl just hoots, mocking me with glee.
A branch gives a wave, I swear it's alive,
I'm pretty sure plants have begun to connive.

The wind has a knack for tickling my nose,
And rustling my hair, it likes to impose.
With a tumble and roll, I trip on a twig,
Those cheeky old leaves, they dance like a jig!

Twilight Among the Trees

In twilight's glance, they dance, so spry,
Whispers of secrets float, oh my!
Squirrels plotting tiny heists,
As shadows tease the moonlit nights.

Branches wag, like arms, they sway,
A frolicsome game, come out to play!
Beneath the stars, the trees regale,
With laughter carried on the gale.

Roots that Speak to Time

In the soil, the roots confide,
Tales of dust, and time that glide.
They giggle softly, roots on parade,
While worms debate the best charade.

Underneath the ground they plot,
A sitcom of dramas, oh, what a lot!
With every twist and every bend,
They argue like an old-time friend.

Flickers of Sun through Thickets

Sunlight pokes through leafy arms,
Playing hide and seek with charms.
Little rays with silly grins,
Tickle the flowers, spin and spin!

Thickets blush with every glance,
Each flicker plays a merry dance.
The wind joins in, a lively tune,
As shadows rhythmically swoon.

Veils of Verdant Grace

Curtains of green, a leafy show,
The trees compose a salsa flow.
Leaves twirl down in dizzying spree,
As branches chuckle, 'Come dance with me!'

In breezy jest, they sway and spin,
With every gust, a new begin!
They wink at passers, a leafy delight,
With playful whispers, fading into night.

Embracing the Emerald

In a suit made of ferns, I prance around,
My friends all laugh, what a sight I've found.
A dandelion hat, a twig for a cane,
I dance with the weeds, oh, what joy and gain!

The squirrels take bets on my leafy attire,
They giggle and chirp, caught up in the fire.
I twirl in the shade, feel the soft, leafy brush,
With each little step, I create quite the hush.

Murmurs of Moss

Mossy cushions beckon for me to recline,
A nature-made couch, isn't it divine?
I host tea parties with the ants in their haste,
While frogs lend their voices, a tune not to waste.

The slugs are my guests, all dressed in their shine,
They slide over carpets of emerald so fine.
I giggle at them—what a humorous sight!
Each nibble they take sparks delightful delight.

Aerial Aria

The branches above me hold whispers of cheer,
As I dance with the breeze, can you hear them near?
They gossip of sunshine, of water and rain,
While I leap and I twirl, delighting in gain.

A parrot comes by, suggests I do tricks,
I flip-flop on branches, away from the ticks.
He clutches a twig, waves regally proud,
Together we sing, creating a cloud.

The Palette of Photosynthesis

I found a new hobby, painting with green,
With fingers dipped in chlorophyll sheen.
I splatter the ground, what a colorful mess,
The bumblebees giggle, they can't help but bless.

The daisies join in, offering vibrant hues,
While sunflowers gossip about last night's blues.
The butterflies flutter, they can hardly believe,
My artistry shines, with tricks up my sleeve.

Symphony of Stalwart Branches

The trees are blushing, a leafy green,
Swaying to tunes that are hardly seen.
Squirrels dance flutes with acorn delight,
While owls conduct from their perch up high.

Raindrops tap like a cheerful drum,
Barking dogs join in, oh what a hum!
Branches bend low, craving the breeze,
As the moon giggles, hiding in trees.

The Secret Life of the Wooded Realm

In a forest so dense, the whispers abound,
Mice wear top hats while teasing the hound.
Fungi throw parties, all spore and cheer,
While beetles moonwalk, no worries here!

Fern fronds gossip of creatures unseen,
Chipmunks in tuxedos, so dapper, so keen.
Rabbits play poker, a game of mischief,
As the sunbeams laugh, with a lighthearted whiff.

Mosaic of Nature's Kaleidoscope

Colors explode in the dappled sun,
Butterflies flutter, oh what fun!
Ladybugs waltz on a live green stage,
While a wise old tree turns the page.

A raccoon in glasses reads tales of yore,
As shadows and sunlight create folklore.
The wind is a jester, tickling the bark,
A day in the woods leaves a joyful mark.

Arborial Dreams and Starlit Nights

Under the canopy, where dreams take flight,
Fireflies twinkle, a soft, glowing sight.
Crickets recite in amusing tones,
As the stars above share their shiny bones.

Branches hang low, like gossiping friends,
Trading tall tales that never quite ends.
Squirrels recount their acorn heists,
While the moon chuckles, rolling in slices.

The Silent Cradle of Green

In a quiet corner, squirrels plot,
Their acorn stash grows in the pot.
A leafy blanket sways around,
Whispering secrets, quite profound.

A chipmunk laughs, a rogue raccoon,
In leafy homes, they sing a tune.
A twig snaps loud, and chaos flies,
As squirrels wear their camo ties.

The bugs hold court on blades of grass,
Debating who can jump the farthest class.
Under the gaze of a dragonfly,
The jury's verdict? 'Let's all try!'

And when the wind will start to dance,
Leaves twirl about in a wild prance.
Nature's circus, who can ignore?
Laughter hidden, at every door.

Stories in the Shade

Under the boughs, the sunbeam's glow,
A raccoon reads what we don't know.
With leafy pages, tales unfold,
Mysteries of acorns, brightly told.

The ants line up for a grand parade,
Marching to where the lemonade's made.
They plot and scheme with tiny might,
To steal a sip before the night.

A snail shares gossip with a bee,
'Did you hear what happened near the tree?'
And butterflies, all dressed in cheer,
Flutter around, 'Did you catch that deer?'

A gentle breeze joins in their fun,
As leaves chuckle, one by one.
In the shade, the stories bloom,
Nature's comedy, a sweet perfume.

The Rustle of Change

When autumn calls, the leaves all grin,
Dancing down while the world spins.
Shiny reds and golds emerge,
As squirrels plan a nutty surge.

The wind teases, takes a jest,
Flinging leaves, it's all a test!
Who can flutter longest, bright?
A game of tag, oh what a sight!

Underfoot, the crunching sound,
With every step, laughter's found.
Squeaky shoes make quite the fuss,
Join the party, ride the bus!

And as the twilight starts to fall,
The leaves giggle, in a ball.
A swirling dance in twilight's twine,
Who can resist this grand design?

Sunlit Canopies

Among the dappled, sunlit beams,
A toad croaks out his silly dreams.
With his crown of moss upon his head,
He rules the logs, at least, he said.

Under the branches, shadows play,
Where critters plot their gentle sway.
They giggle soft as sunlight streams,
In games of hide and seek, it seems.

Behind the bark, the chatter's loud,
A family of beetles feeling proud.
They roll their ball, it's made of leaves,
While watching clouds, they share their eaves.

As day gives way to starry nights,
The moon will dance with leaf's delights.
A twilight show, just wait and see,
A leafy stage for you and me.

The Breath of Branches

In the breeze they do waltz, so spry,
Dancing trees, reaching for the sky.
A squirrel stumbles, takes a dive,
Claims the floor, declares, "I thrive!"

Gusty whispers tickle bark,
Routine meetings after dark.
The branches gossip, branch to branch,
Plotting a way to make us prance.

Oh, to be a leaf in spring!
Free to tease, float, bounce, and swing.
But they scream and flutter with glee,
"Watch us outshine that old apple tree!"

In autumn, colors go bold and bright,
A fashion show that ends in flight.
They sprinkle down with reckless spree,
Saying, "Catch us if you can, we're free!"

Swaying Silhouettes

Under the moon, they gently sway,
Casting shadows, come what may.
A dance-off starts with a twig twist,
Branches shout, "You can't resist!"

A parrot lounges, giggles gleam,
Joining the party, it's quite the scene.
"Oh, my leaves! Is that a breeze?"
"Nope, just us cutting loose with ease!"

Bouncing with laughter, they share their tunes,
Harmonizing with the cheeky raccoons.
The light shows off a leafy parade,
Nature's quirkiest promenade!

As daylight creeps upon the night,
Branches strike a pose—what a sight!
But let us not forget this gist:
They laugh as the humans try to assist.

Harmonies of the Hardwood

With every rustle, a tale unfolds,
The trunks are wise, the young ones bold.
"Oak, do tell, what's your grand plan?"
"Napping all day—best way, man!"

A chorus of chirps fills the air,
Critters unite, no room for despair.
Each critter's quirk a part of the song,
"Hey, you tripped! Come join the throng!"

Beneath the boughs, a banquet awaits,
Mice serve cheese, it's a party of mates.
Leaves clap hands, and branches chime,
Paying tribute to nature's rhyme.

As sunlight fades, the giggles grow,
Swaying joyfully to the glow.
Under the stars, they spin and twirl,
Nature's fun fest, give it a whirl!

The Quietude of Quercus

In the woods where whispers glide,
Quercus grins with leafy pride.
His branches arch, a comfy seat,
"Got snacks up here, come take a seat!"

The chipmunks gather, unable to hide,
Sharing secrets to which he's tied.
"Did you hear the one about the breeze?"
"It tickles the branches - makes them sneeze!"

Bacteria giggle from below,
Providing nutrients in steady flow.
"Oak, you're sprouting a funny new leaf!"
"Just a phase, don't spread that belief!"

Through seasons of change, they revel and play,
Nature's comedy at the end of the day.
And as the dusk settles, a last giggle sounds,
Grand tales of the outdoors spread wide around.

The Artistry of Arbor

In the garden, they sway so free,
Talking trees with gossip like tea.
Branches twist in a silly dance,
Leafy laughter, given a chance.

Underneath, the critters conspire,
Squirrels plotting, never tire.
Rustling tales of wind and flight,
Nature's mischief, what a sight!

Sunshine paints their faces bright,
Shadows play in the soft twilight.
Each leaf giggles, catching a breeze,
Tickling secrets from branches with ease.

When fall comes, they'll drop with grace,
Some will twirl, while others race.
A leafy mess on the ground they'll make,
Oh, what fun, for laughter's sake!

Vibrations of the Vines

Creeping up the garden wall,
Vines have secrets, hear their call.
Whispered jokes from twisting trails,
Giggling leaves tell funny tales.

Between the trellises they play,
A leafy band, they swing and sway.
Grapes are laughing, swelling wide,
A comedy show, nature's pride.

On sunny days, they bask and joke,
Tangled friends, a leafy cloak.
When the rain falls, splashes abound,
Splashing giggles all around.

With every snip, a vine will tease,
A playful dance upon the breeze.
In green attire, they flaunt their tricks,
Charming us all with nature's mix!

A Celestial Canopy

Under the sky, the branches spread,
A blanket woven where dreams are fed.
Birds chirp jokes, a comedic show,
On leafy stages, they steal the flow.

Clouds drift by, they poke and tease,
Sprinkling sunlight with playful ease.
High above, the leaves all sigh,
"Watch the world spin and curl, oh my!"

The wind joins in with a howling cheer,
While squirrels laugh, their antics near.
From acorns to apples, there's fun to find,
The celestial canopy too, intertwined.

As twilight calls, colors ablaze,
Fading laughter, a warm, soft haze.
In moonlit glow, they twinkle bright,
A family of leaves, what pure delight!

Graced by Greenery

Down by the garden, the greens all chat,
With swaying hips, and a leafy spat.
Lettuce giggles, while cabbage sighs,
"Did you hear about those flying pies?"

Herbs start humming a tuneful song,
Dancing together, they all get along.
Rosemary's twirling, mint's doing flips,
Every plant sports its best party tips.

When the sun sets, they slow their pace,
In the clubhouse, they keep good grace.
Under the stars, they share a snack,
"Who knew our laughter could fill a whole pack?"

Even at dusk, the humor runs deep,
In a patch of green, at home they keep.
Graced by the greenery, bound by the fun,
Learning each day, while basking in sun!

Reverie Amongst the Flora

In a garden where daisies wear hats,
The gnomes hold debates, ignore the spats.
A rabbit in glasses takes notes with flair,
While squirrels are plotting world domination there.

Sunflowers nodding, agreeing with bees,
An argument brews 'tween the roots and the leaves.
They gossip of roses, so proud in their beds,
While worms dance a jig on their unbothered heads.

The ladybugs twirl, quite the sight to behold,
As butterflies giggle, their wings made of gold.
A cactus recites all the puns he can find,
It's clear in this garden, they're all a bit blind.

But just as they cheer, a storm rolls on in,
The wind steals the hats, and the laughter grows thin.
Yet through the chaos, the flowers still greet,
In this fun little jungle, life's often a treat.

The Poetry of Decay

A leaf once so green, now wears wrinkles and brown,
Complains to the tree, 'I'm the talk of the town!'
Grumpy old acorns are falling from grace,
While mushrooms hold court at a very odd pace.

The compost brigade, they gather with cheer,
With echoes of laughter, and enough dirt to smear.
'We'll stack up the layers, make magic with smell,
It's a banquet for bugs, can you hear them all yell?'

The vine's losing grip, it's a slippery race,
As worms on a mission make quite a disgrace.
They wriggle and giggle, creating a mess,
In the dance of decay, they truly are blessed.

Yet through all the muck, there's a beauty so bright,
In this symphony of rot, they take flight.
For in every old leaf that's turned into snacks,
Life's poetry flourishes, and great joy it backs.

Whispers of the Wind through Green

The breeze tells a joke to the cherry tree grand,
It's spreading the laughter across the land.
'Your blossoms are cute, but they have a short lease,
Maybe try out a hat? It could bring you some peace!'

The vines all entwine, whisper sweet nothings,
Dreaming of fig pies and other sweet flings.
But the butterflies giggle, their dance quite absurd,
While trying to debate what the flowers all heard.

In the shade of the oaks, the critters recline,
Comparing their tales, sipping sun's brilliant shine.
A fox shares a story, none quite takes the bait,
For when it comes to foxes, do they ever relate?

As the wind continues, it tumbles and plays,
With secrets and laughter, it carries our days.
Whispers of nature, a chatty old friend,
In this world of green, where the fun never ends.

Beneath the Green Horizon

Under the canopies, the critters convene,
To strategize snacks, keep the pantry clean.
A snail swears he'll race, but he's stuck on a leaf,
It's hard to be quick when you're covered in grief.

Frogs croak like poets, in rhymes far too bold,
With tales of the pond and its treasures untold.
But when the clumsy hare comes jumping around,
It's a comedy show when he lands on the ground!

A grasshopper leaps, makes a bet with a bee,
'Let's dance till we tire, and see who's more free.'
But mid-air he flops, landing right on a shoe,
The bee rolls with laughter, as he buzzes on through.

Yet, look to the sunset, the branches all sway,
As nature's laughter keeps worries at bay.
Calls of the wild, mixed with giggles so fine,
Beneath the green horizon, all mischief's divine.

Mosaic of Moss

In a patch of green, they gather round,
Mossy like slippers, they've found their ground.
A party of ferns with a splash of fun,
Wobbling and giggling beneath the sun.

Chasing the raindrops, they leap and twirl,
Dancing with pebbles, they spin and whirl.
A sneaky old snail tries to join the spree,
But he's just too slow for such jubilee.

They throw little hats made of acorn caps,
While frogs give a croak, "Watch out for the mishaps!"
Each leaf a dancer in nature's delight,
Under the moon, they'll groove through the night.

The trees shake their branches, a whimsical cheer,
"Come join the giggles; the time is near!"
In the mosaic of moss, life's a big jest,
Where even the lichen serves as a guest.

Arcane Arbor Chronicles

In the shady woods, they plot and scheme,
The squirrels form bands; it's a nutty dream.
With branches as trumpets, they start to croon,
An arcane tune under the watchful moon.

Following whispers in the rustling leaves,
They conjure up mischief, as the night weaves.
A twig becomes a wand, magically bright,
Turning raindrops to pearls with sheer delight.

The raccoons wear masks, oh what a sight!
Stealing the scenes, they're the stars of the night.
With shadows like capes, they take center stage,
An arcane dance on the forest's great page.

As dawn starts to break, the tale's not done,
They nap in the sun, all the mischief and fun.
Awake with a yawn, they'll start it anew,
In the chronicles where the wild things grew.

Palette of Shadows

In the dappled light, the shadows play tricks,
A palette of green, they pull silly picks.
The branches are brushes; the leaves are the hues,
Stirring up laughter, with nature's own cues.

A vine takes a turn, like a snake in disguise,
While critters applaud with big, winky eyes.
Each step's a caper, each leap is a jest,
In shadows that flicker, they find joy impressed.

A wanderer's hat, made of petals and twine,
Sails through the air, dancing like fine wine.
The squirrels take bets on which way it will go,
For in this grand game, they steal the show.

As twilight descends, the giggles subside,
From the palette of shadows, they scatter with pride.
Tomorrow, they promise, the fun won't be shy,
For laughter brandishes wings, ready to fly.

The Melody of Maple

In a thick of maples, the music erupts,
With notes in the breeze, even the sap interrupts.
A symphony of rustles, a light-hearted sound,
The notes leap and twist, as joy does abound.

The woodpecker drums on a hollowed-out tree,
While the crows join the chorus, oh how carefree!
They take to the air, in a synchronized spree,
Who knew trees could dance? It's a sight to see!

The leaves flutter down like confetti of gold,
While the chipmunks and acorns all boost the bold.
Nature's own band, cheers of laughter ring clear,
In the melody of maple, the fun draws near.

As stars peek above and silence takes hold,
They hum nature's tune, a secret retold.
Tomorrow will bring more joyful display,
In the melody of maple, life's a fun play.

Echoes in the Underbrush

In the thicket, something stirs,
A squirrel chuckles, justice blurs.
Beneath the branches, secrets peek,
A raccoon pranks, it's quite unique.

The whispers dance, a song so bold,
A badger hums, while stories unfold.
The mushrooms giggle at passing feet,
As ants march by, they can't take a seat.

With every rustle, a tiny joke,
The breeze plays tricks, it loves to poke.
Nature's laughter, a symphony bright,
In the underbrush, pure delight!

A Tapestry of Bark and Petals

Fluffy caterpillars strut with flair,
While petals blush, they don't care a hair.
A beetle taps, it feels so slick,
In this patch, humor does the trick.

The flowers giggle, blades of grass sway,
As bees buzz by, they're here to play.
A ladybug's hat looks quite absurd,
It's the fanciest insect, oh how I've heard!

Tangled roots weave stories so nice,
Whispers of laughter roll like dice.
Nature's quilt of color and glee,
In this funny patch, just let it be!

The Breath of the Forest Floor

Oh, what's that sound? A wiggle and sway,
Tiny critters dance night and day.
The ground chuckles, in silence it strives,
With every step, the forest thrives.

Mushrooms bow, like a funny show,
While dampened leaves scatter below.
A worm rolls by in a top hat style,
Twirling around with a wriggly smile!

Under the roots, a disco ball glows,
All the fungi join in with glorious throes.
Nature's antics, all around we adore,
On this jolly, bustling forest floor.

Shadows of the Leafy Mirage

In the dappled sun, a shadow prances,
Leaves whisper tales, and the breeze enhances.
A fox with glasses reads a book,
In this leafy realm, let's take a look!

Amidst the boughs, shadows play tricks,
With squirrels in suits, throwing quick flicks.
A rabbit's dance, oh what a sight,
In the leafy mirage, everything's bright!

Laughter echoes through branches high,
Underneath the watchful sky.
In this woodland wonder, joy outpours,
As shadows frolic, and fun restores!

Palette of the Seasons

In a world where colors play,
Each hue has something funny to say.
Yellow giggles, green does a dance,
While orange insists on wearing pants!

Red tells jokes, such a vibrant clown,
While purple keeps spinning, won't sit down.
Brown offers hugs, big and goofy,
As black rolls the dice, feeling quite boofy!

Leaves wear crowns, they twirl about,
Chasing the wind, they'll scream and shout.
Every fall's a festive parade,
With colors that dance, never afraid!

So here's to the palette we'd never trade,
In this breezy ball, our laughter made.
Together we sway, a colorful team,
In nature's party, we reign supreme!

Trill of the Trees

Listen closely, hear the trees,
Whispering secrets on the breeze.
One dressed in leaves, an awkward dress,
Sways to a tune, sent to impress!

Another shimmies, a branchy twist,
Claiming it's part of an artist's list.
With every rustle, they let out a cry,
A chorus of laughter drifting by!

Skinny trunks hold up their heads,
While round ones giggle, rolling spreads.
With roots in a tangle, they trip and fall,
Yet all they do is laugh, through it all!

So join the trill, the arboreal beat,
As trees share jokes in a leafy seat.
With every chuckle, the forest will cheer,
In this woodsy giggle fest, we have no fear!

Harbor of Hues

In the harbor where colors dock,
Red boats joke, while yellow rocks.
Blue waves giggle, splashing fun,
As orange sails bask in the sun!

Green teaches the crew to dance,
While purple boats pull off a prance.
Each shade's a sailor, wild and free,
In this colorful world, just wait and see!

The hues all gather, making a scene,
Painting the waves with a splashy sheen.
They trade their stories of wind and rain,
Each tale more wacky, quite hard to explain!

So float along in this vibrant bay,
Where laughter echoes throughout the day.
Join the crew for a color spree,
In the harbor of hues, all crazy and free!

Shelters of Sycamores

Under the sycamores, life's a blast,
Leaves sprinkle laughter, moving fast.
Swinging low, they're telling tales,
Of how they fought off wild gales!

One claimed it danced with a daring crow,
While others rolled down, a leaf parade show.
With every twist and playful fall,
They share their fun, one and all!

Branches offer shade for games of tag,
Leaves peek through, giving a wag.
They sing and chat as breezes hum,
Creating a place where good vibes come!

So gather 'round this leafy space,
In sycamores' arms, find your place.
With joy in the air, let laughter soar,
In the sheltering arms of the sycamores!

Secrets in the Shade

Underneath the tree's wide hat,
Squirrels gossip, oh so fat.
They share tales of acorn he'll,
And the daring dance of a daffodil.

A robin's laugh is hard to miss,
Sipping nectar, blissful bliss.
While ants march on, a little parade,
Plotting mischief in the glade.

Under the bough, the shadows play,
Twirling leaves like a cabaret.
Every rustle, a secret told,
In this kingdom of green and gold.

So if you stroll beneath this scene,
Expect the gossip, but don't intervene.
For who knows what tales may sprout,
When nature's laughter dances about?

Rustling Dreams

Whispers swirl in leafy crowns,
As breezes play, the laughter pounds.
A leaf takes flight, a kite on high,
Chasing clouds in the bluest sky.

Acorns tumble, giggles burst,
While critters claim their quirkiest first.
Pine needles drop like confetti rain,
Celebrating life, it's never a pain!

A wooden swing hangs, creaking cheer,
With every squeak, we draw near.
Who knew branches could jest so loud?
Nature's own, the silliest crowd!

So come join the leaf-filled glee,
Where rustling dreams want to be free.
A playful dance, a joyful cheer,
In this green party, have no fear!

Poetry of the Petiole

Petiole swaying, trying to rhyme,
With each gust of wind, it thinks it's sublime.
Branches bend while they recite,
A sonnet to the moon, a whimsical sight.

"Hey, did you hear?" the leaves all chime,
"Where's the sun? He's running behind!"
They giggle and shake, a leafy parole,
In the theater of nature, they play their role.

A breeze brings laughter, quite a hit,
As berries joke about their pit.
The dance of foliage, a merry jest,
In this vibrant haven, they're truly blessed.

So listen close, let the rhythm flow,
Among the green, let your spirits grow.
For in the rustle and sway, you'll find,
The petiole's poem is never maligned!

Heartbeats in the Grove

In the grove where giggles bloom,
Heartbeats echo, chasing gloom.
Frogs play drums on lily pads,
While dancing ants are all just fads.

A plume of grass twirls, saying "Hey!"
Tickling toes on a sunny day.
Leaves are whispering sweet nothings bright,
As butterflies join in for delight.

"Who's there?" croaks the wise old toad,
"Just us leaves, on humor's road!"
They chuckle and waver, such a sight,
In the heart of the grove, everything's bright.

So come dance 'neath the emerald skies,
With heartbeats thumping, a sweet surprise.
For joy abounds in every shade,
In this grove where memories are made!

The Color of Connection

In the park, I wore green socks,
My neighbor laughed, thought I was a fox.
We danced like trees, swayed all around,
While squirrels giggled at us, profoundly profound.

A leaf fell down, it landed on my nose,
I sneezed so loud, it scared the crows!
They cawed and cackled, in a comical way,
As I tripped on my laces and rolled in the hay.

The maple said, 'Oh, what a sight!'
'You clumsy human, take flight!'
I laughed along, with a chuckle and cheer,
For nature knows how to tickle with mirth sincere.

And when the autumn winds start to dance,
I'll wear my socks and take a chance.
For every leaf that whirls and spins,
Is a reason to smile, and let joy begin.

Hues of Hope

Yellow bright, like a morning's first light,
Paints my breakfast, what a curious sight!
Avocados and toast with berries galore,
Even the fridge says, 'Let's explore!'

Orange peels glisten, a citrusy zest,
I slipped on a peel, I must confess.
With a giggle that echoed through the kitchen wide,
A dance with the citrus was hard to confide.

Red leaves tumble, like clowns in a ring,
They somersault down while the birds start to sing.
A parade of colors, all laugh and cheer,
As I join in their folly, without any fear.

So here's to colors, bold and bright,
They brighten our days, fill us with delight.
In this colorful world, we'll dance and we'll sway,
With a laugh and a song to chase gloom away.

Beneath Buoyant Boughs

Under a tree, I took my seat,
A squirrel leaped by, oh what a feat!
He rode the branches like a pro,
With a flick of his tail, he put on a show.

Beneath those branches, shadows play,
I tried to nap, but they said, 'No way!'
The gentle breeze tickled my ear,
As if nature whispered, 'You're not welcome here!'

A chipmunk laughed, as I tried to snooze,
He gathered his nuts and shared his news.
'The acorns are ripe, come join in the fun!'
I giggled and rolled, saying, 'Oh, why not run?'

So, under boughs where the laughter flows,
I found that life's silly, as everyone knows.
With each rustling leaf and cheeky chime,
We celebrate moments, one giggle at a time.

The Fairytale of Foliage

Once in a forest, so lively and green,
A leaf dreamed big, oh what a scene!
'I'll be a crown for a princess so sweet,'
But she lost her grip and fell at my feet.

The owls would hoot tales of charm and of flair,
As raccoons plotted schemes in the moonlit air.
A wise old tree said, 'Don't fret, little sprout,
In this fairytale world, you'll always stand out!'

The petals would giggle, 'You're not alone,'
In this merry tale, the forest has grown.
With laughter like sunlight, they danced in a ring,
While a butterfly shouted, 'Let's all join and sing!'

So here in the woods, where the wild things play,
The fairytale of foliage brightens the day.
In every nook, there's a jest or a jive,
And the spirit of fun is surely alive!

A Journey Through the Jungle

In the jungle, I trip on a vine,
A parrot squawks, saying I'm fine.
Monkeys swing, making a fuss,
While I stumble, oh what a plus!

The sloths cheer me on, oh so slow,
Chasing my tail, can you believe the show?
Leaves fall down like confetti, you see,
I'm the star in this wild comedy!

A toucan laughs, feathers a-go,
With a beak like a rainbow, oh what glow!
Every step feels like a dance,
Nature's whimsy, I take a chance!

When I finally find my way back home,
I'll tell my tale, not to roam!
The jungle's laughs forever now cling,
To my heart, oh what fun they bring!

The Serenity of Sap

The trees are chatting, what a delight,
With syrupy sap oozing just right.
A squirrel slips in a sticky embrace,
Leaves giggle, oh what a place!

Bees buzz in chorus, with rhythm divine,
Pollinating gossip over sugary wine.
Stickiness leads to an awkward mess,
But nature smiles, more joy to express!

A woodpecker drums in a silly beat,
Echoes of laughter, impossible to defeat.
With each whack, a joke takes flight,
In this sweet sap party, everything's bright!

So when life gets sticky, dance around,
Like the leaves that twirl upon the ground.
Join the fun and relish the trap,
In the serenity of nature's sap!

Voices of the Verdant

In the forest, a rustle breaks the calm,
A chipmunk sings, oh isn't that charm?
The ferns sway, moving like they groove,
Nature's concert—really, who needs to prove?

The willow waves with a gentle tease,
"Hello there!" it whispers through the breeze.
A cacophony of chatter fills the air,
Who knew leaves could gossip and care?

With every shiver, a joke is spun,
Laughter spreads like rays from the sun.
When the flowers gossip, oh what a show,
They bloom in colors, let the humor flow!

So in this green realm, join the jest,
Embrace the chuckles, let them invest.
In the voices of the verdant, we find cheer,
Nature's laughter is always near!

Lush Legacy

A legacy written in shades of green,
Lush laughter echoes, a joyous scene.
Each leaf tells a tale, quirky and bright,
Of a branch that danced all through the night!

The daisies wink in their sunny cheer,
While the grass tickles toes that wander near.
A garden plot filled with secrets untold,
Comedic mishaps like gold that unfold!

Bouncing bunnies with silly hops,
Creating chaos where the fun never stops.
The tomato plants boast of their red,
While cucumbers giggle, raising their heads!

So in this lush land, where humor holds sway,
Let's laugh with each leaf, come what may.
For in the abundance, we find we belong,
In the legacy of laughter, we'll always be strong!

Echoes of Eucalyptus

In the breeze, they rustle loud,
Whispers of trees, a funny crowd.
Barking up jokes on sunny days,
Eucalyptus giggles in quirky ways.

Squirrels dance in leafy heights,
Chasing shadows, they share their flights.
Branches tease with a playful sway,
Leaves are laughing, come what may!

Twirling in their green attire,
Branching out, they never tire.
With every drop of morning dew,
A chuckle shared by just a few!

As the sun dips, colors collide,
Nature's humor, our happy guide.
Eucalyptus knows the punchline here,
Join the laughter, spread the cheer!

A Tapestry of Treasures

Foliage bright, a greenish quilt,
Stitching laughs with no guilt.
Pinecones slide on the forest floor,
Nature's marbles, a playful score.

Gathering acorns in silly hats,
Chittering squirrels, what acrobat!
Maple leaves wiggle in a jig,
Dancing round in a leafy gig.

Sunlight trickles through leaf veins,
Tickling ferns, breaking chains.
Each rustle tells a jokester's tale,
In this grove, humor will prevail.

A tapestry spun, we weave delight,
In the forest, all's just right.
Laughter echoes, a treasure we find,
In the embrace of the leafy kind!

The Symphony of Saplings

Tiny trees, a quirky band,
Making music across the land.
Their branches wiggle, roots go deep,
In harmony, they sing and leap.

A chorus of leaves, bright and spry,
With giggles shared beneath the sky.
Saplings sway, no need for fear,
Nature's jesters, always here.

They tickle clouds and poke the sun,
Joyful shivers, oh what fun!
Whistling winds join in the spree,
Creating tunes underneath the trees.

Take a listen, what do you hear?
Nature's laughter, crystal clear.
The symphony plays, come join the chat,
In fun and foliage, let's all have a chat!

Green Reveries

In the garden, dreams take flight,
Leaves are giggling, what a sight!
Marigolds join, sporting their crowns,
Swaying with laughter, they never frown.

Grapes are grinning, hanging down,
Plump with joy, they own the town.
Cabbage twirls in playful cheer,
A veggie party drawing near.

The daisies shout with sheer delight,
Tickling tulips in morning light.
Frogs croak jokes in the pond so clear,
Green reveries, the path sincere.

With every bloom, let laughter rise,
In the kaleidoscope of verdant skies.
Nature's humor, forever plays,
In green reveries, our hearts amaze!

Stories in Shadows

In shadows deep, the critters prance,
Squirrels twirl, their acorn dance.
A rabbit hops, with quite the flair,
While chatting trees spill tales in air.

A fox, in denim, with a hat askew,
Winks at a crow, who thinks he's cool.
They scheme and laugh, what a silly sight,
In the dappled shade, from morning to night.

A beetle boasts about his ride,
On a fallen leaf, oh what a glide!
The shadows tell jokes, so loud and clear,
Nature's stand-up, year after year.

So listen closely, when the sun dips low,
To the whispers of shadows that put on a show.
For in leafy laughter, life's stories unfold,
A comedic tale, that never gets old.

The Warmth of Woodlands

In the woods, the trees conspire,
To tickle the breeze and make it higher.
A lumberjack laughs, with his chainsaw's song,
"Why did the log break? It did nothing wrong!"

A picnic's laid where the sun beams bright,
Ants march in line, a curious sight.
"Hey, that cupcake's mine!" they seem to yell,
As they form a line, oh what a smell!

Bears with bow ties, sipping on tea,
With a dash of honey, oh what glee!
They gossip and chuckle, a raucous scene,
In the warm woodland, where life's a dream.

So, next time you wander through leafy splendor,
Remember the mischief, let joy be your tender.
In the warmth of woodlands, fun fills the air,
With laughter and folly, beyond all compare.

The Texture of Tensile

Stretching branches in the breeze,
Waving at the bumblebees.
"Can you touch your toes?" a twig does tease,
While the grassgiggles, "We do as we please!"

Caterpillars flex, like little gyms,
Testing their strength on fragile limbs.
"Who's the strongest, shall we compete?"
The vines chimed in, "We can't be beat!"

A sturdy oak, shakes with glee,
"I wore these leaves since '53!"
Laughter in rustles, a joyous spree,
In this playful world, how grand it can be.

So let's stretch those roots, stand tall and proud,
And dance with the wind, oh let's shout loud!
For the texture of tensile wraps us with cheer,
In nature's embrace, we hold nothing dear.

The Sanctuary of Saplings

Tiny sprouts laugh, in a row,
"Look out for worms, they're putting on a show!"
Saplings sway, like little kids,
Jumping in puddles, oh what skids!

In the sanctuary, stories bloom,
"Tell me a tale, it's a bit too gloom!"
They spin tales of stars, and moonlit nights,
While leaves join in, with fluttering flights.

A hedgehog hums, 'neath a bramble bush,
With its cozy home, there's no need to rush.
A chorus of peas, green and proud,
Sings with the breeze, lively and loud.

So step into this haven, where giggles play,
In the sanctuary of saplings, joy's here to stay.
Where each little leaf, has a role to sing,
In a world so silly, it makes all hearts spring.

Journey through the Jungle

In the jungle where we tread,
Parrots squawk like they are fed.
Monkeys swing with playful cheer,
While I trip on roots right near.

Vines hang low, a playful tease,
I duck and dodge, oh please, oh please!
A crocodile with toothy grin,
Laughs at my awkward chagrin.

Swinging lianas, slippery ground,
What a circus I've found!
But laughter echoes through the trees,
As bugs tickle my knees with ease.

With every step in this wild spree,
I find humor hiding in a tree.
So off I dance, glide, and prance,
In this jungle of chance and circumstance.

Timelessness of Treetops

High above where whispers roam,
The squirrels claim their leafy home.
Time slows down in green embrace,
As branches sway, they set the pace.

A raccoon dons a leafy hat,
While birds gossip, imagine that!
And time forgot its rush and race,
In this leafy, slow-paced place.

As I peek through the verdant veil,
A wise old owl shares a tale.
With every hoot, a chuckle shared,
In treetops high, no one is scared.

So here I sit, my heart at ease,
Chuckling with the buzzing bees.
For up above, in skies so bright,
Time's just a joke in leafy light.

The Interlude of Ivy

Ivy creeping up the walls,
In this game, it never falls.
With each twist and knot it weaves,
It plays tricks like mischievous thieves.

"Hello, I'm your neighbor now!"
Said the ivy, taking a bow.
Wrapping round without a care,
My windows welcome leafy flair.

It tickles stones and bricks alike,
A green comedian on a hike.
Sprouting jokes in every crack,
"Did you miss me? I'm back, I'm back!"

As seasons change and colors blend,
The ivy laughs, a quirky friend.
In this dance, we joke and shine,
Together tangled, feeling fine.

Brushstrokes of the Breeze

A gentle breeze plays tricks with leaves,
Whispering secrets, it never grieves.
With every gust, a swirly dance,
Leaves laugh and twirl in a leafy trance.

"Catch me if you can!" they tease,
As I stumble chasing, with ease.
But the wind just giggles and sighs,
As laughter rustles through the skies.

Like paintbrush strokes 'cross canvas wide,
The breeze and leaves take us for a ride.
Tickling noses, sweeping by,
In this playful jest, oh my!

So here I stand, under the glee,
While leaves play tag, just wait for me!
With each interaction, wild and free,
I find joy in this leafy spree.

Choreography of the Foliage

A dance of greens with swirling flair,
The wind's a DJ, spinning air.
Branches shimmy and twirl with glee,
Leaves join in, like they're on TV.

Acorns tumble, like they're on stage,
Making the squirrels laugh, such a rage!
Pine needles do the cha-cha slide,
While moss giggles, barely can hide.

Puffs of dandelion float in sync,
Jigging past, as if to wink.
Nature's rhythm, a quirky bliss,
Who knew a leaf could dance like this?

Joyful foliage, not a care in sight,
They'll boogie until the fall's first night.
In this green ballet, life's just a show,
Grab a front row seat, don't be slow!

Conversations in the Breeze

Two leaves whispering, 'What's the news?',
"Did you hear about the wind's new shoes?"
They giggle lightly, a fluttering sound,
While squirrels chuckle and scurry around.

A branch pipes up, "I'm feeling bold,
Let's throw a party; the world's our gold!"
"Count me in!" hollers a cheeky twig,
"Just make sure to invite that mockingbird gig!"

Rustling voices, nature's own jest,
"Hey, gather 'round, it's a leaf-fest!"
Chatter grows louder, the trees start to sway,
With drumming roots to the laughter's ballet.

The breeze carries tales of who kissed who,
A butterfly swoons over morning dew.
As the sun smiles down, they share and tease,
Conversations bubbling in light summer breeze.

Where Nature's Polaroids Gather

Sunlight snapshots on leafy skin,
Nature's selfies where the fun begins.
Each rustle a memory, a fleeting catch,
Snap for the birds, a brightening patch.

Caught in a breeze, the moment's so right,
A leaf tries to flex, what a sight!
"Quick, hold it there!" cries out a bee,
"Say 'buzz' everyone, smile with glee!"

Critters pose, what a goofy lot,
A squirrel throws nuts, give it a shot!
With each click, a giggle shared,
These goofy gatherings, no one's impaired.

Fleeting shots of laughter in trees,
Where nature's moments come crazy with ease.
So snap your heart out, don't let it pass,
In this wild photo booth, all joy amassed!

Serpentine Trails through Glades

Winding paths of leafy delight,
Squirrels maneuver with questionable might.
Branches above stretch and sway,
As they play hide and seek, come what may!

Twisting and turning, oh what a ride!
Nature's rollercoaster, let's glide!
Just watch your step, or you might see,
A leaf in your shoe, laughing with glee!

Pine cones tumble, roll with a flair,
"Watch out!" bark shouts, "Here's the scare!"
But laughter echoes through each glade,
No mood too serious, all games are played.

Through the snickers and rustles we roam,
On trails of whimsy, we find our home.
In this leafy labyrinth, smiles trail behind,
Winding ever onward, pure cheer designed!

Conversations with Canopies

Under the branches, we start to chat,
Leaves rustle, like a furry acrobat.
"Did you hear?" whispers a curious sprig,
"Squirrels are planning a dance, so big!"

A branch shakes gently, the gossip spreads,
"A snail's new hat is made of shredded threads!"
The sunlight giggles, the shadows play,
As nature shares jokes in its quirky way.

Sometimes they argue, like siblings do,
"Don't steal my sunlight!" says the tall and the blue.
Yet, when the wind comes, they all agree,
Tickling together, so joyfully free.

The tallest tree cracks a pun, oh my!
"Why did the leaf never say goodbye?
Because it thought it was too rooted here!"
And all the canopies erupt with cheer!

The Green Guard

In my backyard stands a leafy knight,
With armor of chlorophyll, oh what a sight!
He guards the garden with a leafy fist,
Chasing away pests with a not-so-mean twist.

A butterfly flutters, making a fuss,
"Why'd you scare me?" she asks with a huff.
The knight replies, "It's my leafy duty,
To keep this patch both cute and fruity!"

The flowers giggle, sharing the news,
"There's a dance tonight, wear your best shoes!"
The knight elbows a bud, "Let's boogie down!"
And all the plants shake it, roots in the ground.

Though twigs might bend, and leaves might sway,
This jolly guard takes work to play.
With laughter echoing through vines and stems,
The garden's alive with whimsical gems!

Grains of Growth

In the moist earth, a seed starts to grin,
Cracking a joke about the shape it's in.
"Why don't we play hide and seek today?
I'll be the seedling, you count, okay?"

As sunlight beams down, they frolic and laugh,
Imagining futures; a tree, maybe half!
"The taller you grow, the worse the view!"
"Don't worry," the sapling yells, "I'll see you!"

A gust of wind shouts, "Time to have fun!"
"Catch me if you can," and off they run!
The grain of growth starts stretching its limbs,
Dancing with gusto, pretending it swims.

The roots intertwine, sharing good vibes,
Swapping secrets of nature's wild tribes.
Giggles disperse as the day softly ends,
In the heart of the earth, where joy transcends!

Evocations of Evergreen

In the evergreen wood, the laughter takes flight,
As branches whisper secrets into the night.
"Oh look!" jokes a pine, "That squirrel's a clown,
He must think he's wearing a leafy crown!"

On a mossy path, the toad hops with zest,
"Word on the street is, I'm nature's best dressed!"
The evergreens chuckle, their needles so proud,
"Join us, dear buddy, come dance with the crowd!"

A brook joins in, singing a bubbly tune,
"No drama here, just a midnight festoon!"
The firs sway along, like dancers in a spree,
As shadows twirl round, so wild and free!

When the morning breaks, all is merry and bright,
With pinecone confetti launching into flight.
The humor unfolds in this timeless grove,
Where every creature sings and laughs in a trove!

www.ingramcontent.com/pod-product-compliance
Lightning Source LLC
Chambersburg PA
CBHW070333120526
44590CB00017B/2867